IT'S AMAZING!
MONSTERS

Annabel Savery

W

FRANKLIN WATTS

Franklin Watts
Published in Great Britain in 2016 by The Watts Publishing Group

Planning and production by Discovery Books Limited
Managing Editor: Laura Durman
Editor: Annabel Savery
Designer: Ian Winton

Dewey number: 001.9'44
ISBN: 978 1 4451 4983 7

Printed in China

Franklin Watts
An imprint of
Hachette Children's Group
Part of The Watts Publishing Group
Carmelite House
50 Victoria Embankment
London EC4Y 0DZ

An Hachette UK company
www.hachette.co.uk

www.franklinwatts.co.uk

CONTENTS

All words in **bold** appear in the glossary on page 30.

WHAT IS A MONSTER?

Have you ever met a monster? Do you ever think there is one under your bed or hiding in your cupboard? It's unlikely because monsters are **imaginary creatures**.

Most monsters have an amazing feature, such as great strength. Some can breathe fire, while others may have two heads.

Many monsters come from old stories called **myths** and **legends**. These have been passed down over hundreds of years by storytellers.

Heroes

Stories about monsters are often used to teach people that good triumphs over bad. The monsters are usually defeated by a great hero. Here, the hero Hercules battles with the fierce Nemean lion.

MYTHICAL MONSTERS

Monster tales began long ago in ancient times. People would tell stories about terrifying creatures that they hoped never to meet!

Greek monsters are fearsome. The Hydra (left) is a many-headed sea monster. There's Cerberus too, the three-headed dog (below). Cerberus is said to guard the gates of the **Underworld**.

Norse monsters are just as terrifying. Fenrir is a huge, fierce wolf. In stories, the gods chain him up but he breaks free.

IT'S AMAZING!

The Chimera is a horrifying Greek monster. It has the body of a lion, a tail that ends in a snake's head and the head of a goat on its back! Luckily, in the myth the hero Bellerophon was able to defeat it with the help of Pegasus the winged horse.

You have probably read about dragons in stories and fairytales.

Traditional dragons are terrifying flying monsters. They have enormous leathery wings, tough scales and clawed feet. Worst of all, they can breathe fire.

In China the dragon is not a fearsome monster but a **symbol** of power, strength and good luck. At festivals, people dress as dragons and parade through the streets.

Real-life dragons

Komodo dragons are the world's largest living lizards. They can be up to three metres long. Komodo dragons are good hunters and can eat animals much bigger than themselves!

Oceans are very wide and deep. They are the perfect place for enormous monsters to hide!

The kraken is a giant squid that lives in the depths of the ocean. It comes from Norwegian **folklore**. In stories, the kraken drags ships below the water and feeds on the sailors.

Real-life monsters live in the sea, too. Sharks are some of the scariest, though few will actually harm you. There are lots of different types of shark.

This is a great white shark. It is one of the largest and deadliest of all the sharks.

IT'S AMAZING!

The whale shark is the biggest fish in the world. It has more than 4,000 teeth, but it uses them to capture the tiny fish it eats. It is a gentle giant.

Reptiles, such as snakes and lizards, can be scary enough. But imagine that they were fifty times bigger and had special powers!

The basilisk (above) is an ancient mythical creature. It is the king of the **serpents** and can kill a person or animal with a single glance.

There are other mythical creatures that are similar to the basilisk. The wyvern (below) has a dragon's head and the tail of a snake.

The cockatrice, in the old drawing below, has the head of a cockerel and the tail of a lizard. Both creatures can also kill with a look.

Boy vs serpent

In *Harry Potter and the Chamber of Secrets*, young wizard Harry fights an enormous basilisk that has been hiding in Hogwarts School for many years.

Many mythical monsters are combinations of different animals. We have seen some of them already!

A griffin (above) has the head and wings of an eagle and the tail and body of a lion. The eagle is king of the birds and the lion is king of the beasts, so the griffin is a very powerful creature.

Centaurs are violent and **unruly** creatures that appear in Greek and Roman myths. They have the chest and head of a human, and the body and legs of a horse.

Centaur Chiron

In Narnia, a land created by author C S Lewis, centaurs are more gentle creatures. They are based on the mythical centaur Chiron, who was noble, wise and powerful.

Some monsters look like enormous or misshapen humans!

Ogres (right) are ugly, huge and strong. They are also usually very unfriendly.

Shrek

The *Shrek* films feature a different sort of ogre. Although Shrek is grumpy, he is also funny, loving and very loyal to his friends.

Trolls (right) are ugly and mean creatures, and they are also a bit stupid. They live in caves, eat people, and sometimes even steal babies. In Scandinavian folklore, trolls turned to stone in sunlight!

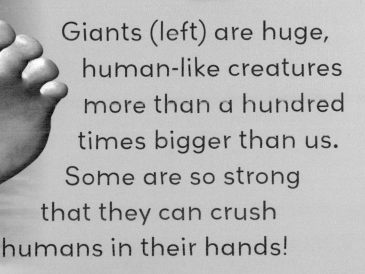

Giants (left) are huge, human-like creatures more than a hundred times bigger than us. Some are so strong that they can crush humans in their hands!

In some stories, monsters are created by people.

In a novel by Mary Shelley, a scientist called Victor Frankenstein creates a new man from the bones and body parts of dead people. Then he brings the monster to life with a spark of lightning!

Frankenstein's monster

The film *Frankenstein* was made in 1931. It is considered one of the best horror films of all time.

The golem (below) is another man-made monster. It comes from traditional Jewish stories.

A golem is a creature made from soil or earth that is brought to life by a human. The golem serves the person who creates it.

Monsters can be very scary. So, take a deep breath and count to ten before reading these pages!

Vampires are creepy creatures. Traditionally, they live forever, drink blood, sleep in coffins, cannot stand daylight and can only be killed with a wooden **stake** through the heart.

Changing vampires

In the *Twilight* series author Stephenie Meyer has changed the traditional idea of vampires. The Cullen family of vampires protect humans, do not drink human blood, never sleep and shimmer like diamonds in sunlight.

Zombies (right) are monsters that were once people. They are dead bodies that have come back to life. Zombies feast on human brains!

Werewolves (left) are people who turn into vicious wolf-like creatures when there is a full moon. One bite from a werewolf and you will become a werewolf, too!

MONSTERS IN MOVIES

Some of the most fantastic monsters appear in films.

King Kong is a giant gorilla. He is captured and taken to New York. Here, he escapes and crashes through the city!

Not so bad!

In the film *Monsters Inc.*, monsters scare children and use the screams to power their city. When a little girl, Boo, gets into the monster world, the monsters discover that laughter is much more powerful than screams. From then on they make children laugh instead!

More amazing monsters were brought to life in the film versions of *The Lord of the Rings* novels. Shelob is an ancient spider-like monster that feeds on **orcs**. The Balrog hides deep below the Misty Mountains and is a fearsome creature made of shadow and fire.

No one knows what might live outside planet Earth. So people use films to imagine what alien monsters might be like.

Gallaxhar (right) is a powerful alien commander in the film *Monsters vs Aliens*. He wants to replace all of the humans on Earth with **clones** of himself!

Aliens on Earth!

The *Men in Black* films (below) starring Will Smith feature lots of scary-looking and unusual aliens. The Men in Black are agents that control aliens on Earth. Crazy creatures are a part of their everyday lives!

The monsters in the *Star Wars* films are really strange. Jabba the Hutt (left) is a huge, slug-like criminal **overlord**. When he is hungry, he slurps down frogs and maggots!

'‘R-AL-LIF-’ M--- T--

Many people around the world think that some monsters are real. They even say that they have seen or found **evidence** of them!

The Loch Ness monster is an enormous snake-like creature said to live in Loch Ness in Scotland. People claim to have taken photos of it (such as the one shown above), but no one can prove that it is actually real.

The yeti (right), also known as the abominable snowman, is said to live in the Himalayan Mountains in Asia. The Yeti is a huge, ape-like monster that walks on two legs and is covered in hair.

Finding monsters

People have set out on expeditions to find the yeti. Some claim to have found footprints, but none have found the actual beasts.

Some of the most monstrous creatures live, or have lived, on the same planet as us.

Some terrifying creatures died out millions of years ago. The smilodon (above) lived during the last Ice Age. It is also called the sabre-toothed tiger. Smilodons were huge, leopard-like animals with extra long, sharp front teeth.

The angler fish (right) lives deep in the ocean and looks like something from a science-fiction film. It attracts prey using a piece of **luminous** skin that dangles in front of its mouth. As soon as a creature gets too close, it strikes with its large, sharp teeth!

IT'S AMAZING!

The venus flytrap plant snaps shut to trap insects that crawl onto it. It then eats the insects. Thank goodness these plants are very small!

clone an exact copy

evidence something that proves something is true

folklore stories and tales from a group of people in a country

imaginary something that is created by the imagination

legend a story that has been handed down from person to person through time

luminous glowing or giving off light

myth a story that comes from a particular tradition, handed down through time

Norse from ancient Scandinavia

orc a fierce human-like creature

overlord a ruler over other people

serpent a snake

stake a sharp, pointed piece of wood

symbol an object or picture that represents something else

Underworld an imaginary world beneath the Earth's surface where spirits live

unruly wild and hard to control

Books

EDGE: Ultimate 20: Beasts and Monsters, Tracey Turner, Franklin Watts.

Tracking Sea Monsters, Bigfoot, and other Legendary Beasts, Nel Yomtov, Capstone Press.

Ready, Set Draw: Monsters and Robots, Paul Gamble, Franklin Watts.

Websites

Find out about some amazing creatures we share the planet with.
crazycreatures.org/

Find out about prehistoric monsters, and watch the National Geographic film *Sea Monsters*.
www.nationalgeographic.com/ seamonsters/kids/

The San Diego Zoo website contains lots of information about Komodo dragons.
animals.sandiegozoo.org/animals/ komodo-dragon

Find out about lots of mythical creatures on the American Museum of Natural History website.
www.amnh.org/explore/ology/ anthropology

Films

Harry Potter and the Chamber of Secrets, Warner Home Video, 2002

King Kong, Universal Pictures UK, 2005

Lord of the Rings; The Fellowship of the Ring (2001), *The Two Towers* (2002), *The Return of the King* (2003), Entertainment in Video

Men in Black, Sony Pictures Home Entertainment, 1997

Men in Black II, Sony Pictures Home Entertainment, 2002

Monsters Inc, Buena Vista Home Entertainment, 2002

Monsters vs Aliens, Dreamworks Home Entertainment, 2009

Star Wars; Prequel Trilogy, 20th Century Fox Home Entertainment, 2008 [*The Phantom Menace* (1999), *Attack of the Clones* (2002), *Revenge of the Sith* (2005)]

Star Wars; The Original Trilogy, 20th Century Fox Home Entertainment, 2008 [*A New Hope* (1977), *The Empire Strikes Back* (1980), *Return of the Jedi* (1983)]

INDEX